Principles of Team Play

by
Allen Wade

Published by
REEDSWAIN, INC.

Library of Congress Cataloging - in - Publication Data

Wade, Allen
    Principles of Team Play/Allen Wade

ISBN No. 09651020-3-3
Copyright © 1996 Allen Wade

Reprinted from the book The F.A. Guide to Training and Coaching with permission from The Football Association.

Reedswain books are available at special discounts for bulk purchase. For details, contact the Special Sales Manager at Reedswain.

Printed in the United States of America.

REEDSWAIN INC
612 Pughtown Road · Spring City PA 19475
1-800-331-5191

Table of Contents

Introduction

There are, reputedly, two stages through which worthwhile ideas must pass before they are accepted. In the first stage they are ignored, in the second, ridiculed. Coaching has passed through these stages and is now accepted as a necessary process in the education and development of more skillful players at all levels. Indeed, if this were not so, the whole process of education from early school years to university level could be viewed with doubts and reservations.

A coach's aim is to find the most economical way of causing a player to become a better player in the widest possible sense. This improvement may relate to the player's understanding of the game or to the development of his technique. More likely it concerns a combination of both: indeed these two aspects of a player's capabilities must be interdependent.

In the past, coaching was ignored because the reservoirs of so-called natural talent seemed limitless. It was subsequently ridiculed, probably because some players, eminent in their time, had not been taught, so it was assumed that no-one could be taught. Had this belief prevailed in the musical field, the development of great instrumentalists would surely have been under a handicap.

This book has been written to present the experience of The Football Association over the years in the fields of coaching and training. The knowledge gained has been, and will continue to be, tested and tried, as new ideas emerge and changes occur. The main purpose of the book is not to provide categorical answers or suggest cut-and-dried methods; answers and methods are not so easily arrived at. Its purpose is to present ideas and principles which will require coaches to think. They, in turn, must provoke thought and enquiry among their players. Unthinking coaches and players mean, ultimately, stagnation in the game. Stagnation produces complacency and this must never again be permitted to occur in this country.

A.W.

Acknowledgment

The Football Association depends upon the unselfish and often unsparing efforts of a great many people for the success of its instructional work. The coaching scheme is the result of the intelligence, skill, and soccer 'know how' of men from all the different levels at which the game is played. To a great extent this book is an attempt to sum up their experience and, as a consequence, my sincere thanks are given to everyone who has contributed to the development of coaching in England. In particular, my thanks are due to the Staff Coaches of The Football Association. These are the men who are responsible for the National Coaching Courses; men who have provided and who continue to provide so much inspiration in the cause of skillful soccer.

The preparation of this book would have been considerably hindered without the cheerful effort lavished upon it by my secretary, Joan Pritchard. To her and to the many others who have assisted me, may I express my gratitude.

Principles of
Team Play

One of the many reasons why soccer is attractive both to players and spectators is its freedom of movement. Attack and defense flow naturally into each other and players can be almost completely unrestricted in their movements on the field of play. The game, then, is basically a free game, but, as in all team games, the aim of a team must be to win the match. This inevitably means the co-ordination of eleven individual efforts into a combined team effort which demands some planning and hence a certain amount of restriction. The planning must be aimed at making the best of each individual's abilities; the restriction involves the calculation of chance, which is an inherent part of the game. It would be ridiculous, for example, to encourage eight players to adopt major attacking roles in order to secure goals if this policy resulted in the opposing team scoring more goals and, therefore, winning the match. There are three principal phases of the game:

1. Attack
2. Defense
3. Preparation or mid-field play

In the third phase neither team has established a complete domination of play, but is involved in re-organization before making an attack or building up its defense.

So far no mention has been made of positions although it is quite clear that certain positions vary in their requirements so far as players are concerned. We, in England, see our teams line up at the kick-off in what is known as the pyramid formation (*fig. 1*).

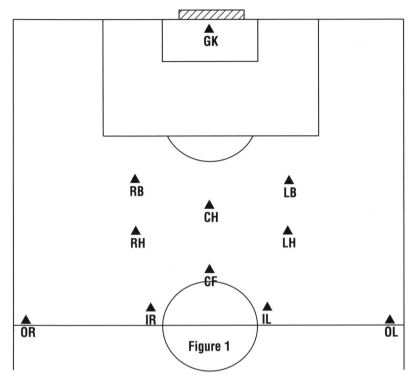

Figure 1

During recent years, however, changes have taken place in this structure. The stopper center-half has been recognized for what he is, a third full-back, and in some countries this is shown both in the opening formation and in the numbering of players (*fig.* 2).

Other countries have adopted a system where there are four 'backs', two 'half-backs' and four 'forwards'. A logical line-up and system of numbering under these circumstances might be that shown in *fig.* 3.

All that this serves to emphasize is that the game is not played by numbers; indeed, the only real significance of numbers is that they serve to identify players in match programs. Unfortunately, this is not always the case in practice; crowds are often bewildered when players in a team appear to be occupying positions bearing no relation to the numbers on their shirts.

There are have been considerable changes in the systems of play developed over the years, and certainly in the tactical use of players. The fact that these developments should attract so much attention is, to some extent, a commentary on a lack of basic understanding on the part of clubs, players, and spectators. Too often, a new system is looked upon as the solution to all

3

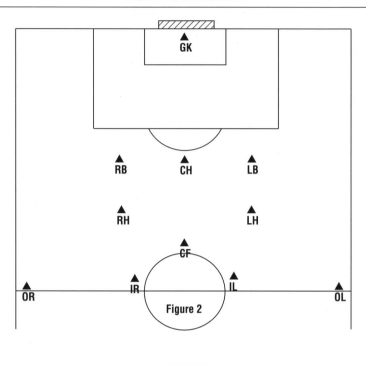

Figure 2

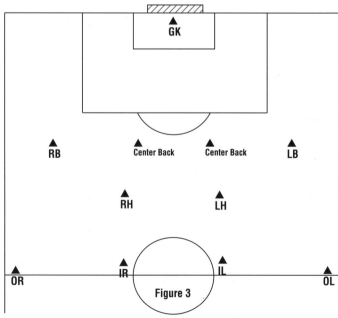

Figure 3

problems. Players are made to fit a system rather than a system being adapted to suit the players. Such a policy inevitably leads to restriction and the creative and imaginative ability of a player is submerged. Eleven basically good soccer players should be able to adopt any system of play to suit the circumstances of the moment.

The basic problem for players and coaches is one of understanding. We must be capable of presenting the game in such a way as to make its problems coherent at all levels. The principles of the game must be the foundation upon which systems of play and tactical considerations are developed.

The most simple consideration is ball possession. Whenever a team loses possession of the ball, all the players in the team must, at the very least, think defensively. Obviously, some will be immediately committed defensively, either in marking opponents tightly, withdrawing in order to provide a solid last line of defense, or actually challenging an opposing player for possession. It is, nevertheless, true that all the players in the team have the main aim of regaining possession of the ball, restricting their opponents' free use of the ball while, at the same time, exposing their own goal to the minimum possible danger. Similarly, when a team has possession of the ball, every member of that team should think positively about attack. It may be, for example, that the right full back finds himself rather remote from play when his own outside left has the ball in the far corner of the field. The right-back's adjustment may be to move much nearer to his opposing winger, thus taking himself away from a central covering position. He does so with two possibilities in mind: if play switches to his side of the field, he can move quickly in support; secondly he has tightened his marking so that if his team loses possession of the ball the opposing team will not have unrestricted scope for passing.

The first and most important principle in soccer is that ball possession determines everything. There are times when risking losing possession is justified due to an opportunity to shoot at goal. The closer it is pressing its opponents' penalty-area, the more a team is justified in taking such a risk. Conversely, the nearer a team is to its own penalty-area, the fewer should be the risks taken. Accuracy and confident control of the ball are basic requirements of players particularly when they gain possession of the ball in defensive positions.

Individually, the basic factors in a player's performance may be stated as follows:

1. Individual skill and technique
2. Understanding (intelligence)
3. Fitness (mental and physical)

No player can afford to miss an opportunity to improve himself in these three aspects of the game. However, technically well equipped as he may be, failure to study and to improve his understanding of the game will render him much less effective as a player.

Ultimately, all tactical considerations depend upon the skill and the technique of each individual player. Similarly each player's fitness will limit the degree to which he is capable of using his technique and skill in developing the team's playing strategy. Psychological fitness is also necessarily linked with the degree of physical fitness and must be acknowledged as such by a coach. These three factors are thus interdependent.

DEPTH IN ATTACK (*fig.* 4)

Generally speaking an attacking movement with depth allows the player with the ball all-round passing opportunities and, therefore, all-round support. In *fig.* 4a where the OR has the ball, he has a full range of passing opportunities to the positions taken up by the supporting players, IR, RH, CF, and RB.

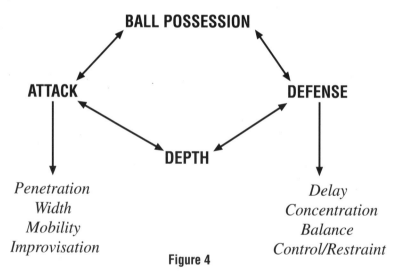

Figure 4

In *fig.* 5 where the Right Half has the ball the forward players have taken up 'flat' positions relative to each other and, presumably, will be closely marked or covered. If two of the forwards moved towards the RH (*fig.* 6) they would increase the passing possibilities open to him and at the same time present problems to the defenders who might be marking them fairly closely. The problem for the defenders is whether or not to follow the

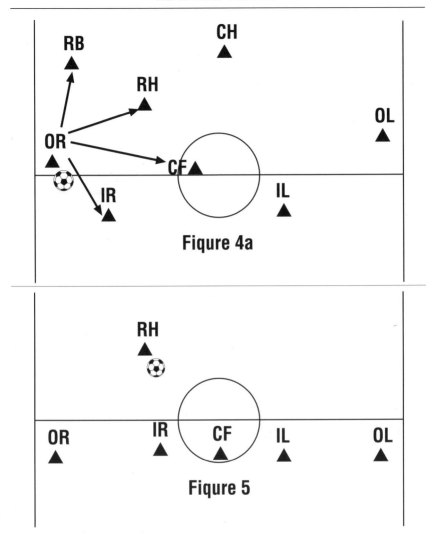

Fiqure 4a

Fiqure 5

attackers. If they follow their attackers they allow space to be created behind them which can be exploited by the RH's use of a through pass. If they remain in covering positions then the opposing attack is allowed a certain degree of freedom in pressing home the attacking movement. Obviously, if there is any real doubt in the minds of the defenders, they will refuse to be drawn into following the attackers.

From the coach's point of view the minimum number of players which can produce depth in attack must be three. They will find themselves in

7

some form of triangular formation, although the nature of this triangle will often change and change rapidly.

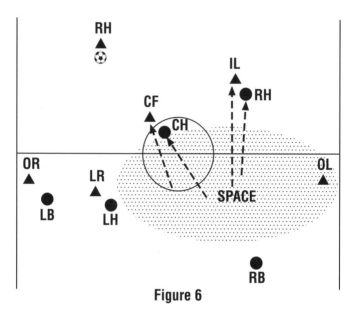

Figure 6

The formation shown in *fig.* 7 shows the OR, IR, and CF attacking in depth. This attack may develop in such a way that the IR sees an opportunity to move into an advanced position. One of the other players will balance the IR's forward run to continue to provide depth, as in *fig.* 8. Here the CF

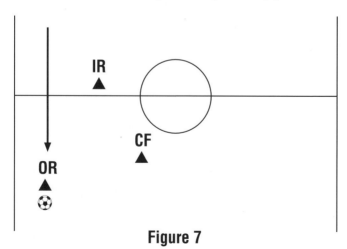

Figure 7

has tried to tempt the CH away from the centre of the field to open up a path or forward runs of the IR, and, having done this, he has folded in behind the other forwards as a supporting player. One can now see why numbers can be misleading in modern soccer, particularly in an attacking phase of the game. The triangle may be pointing in any direction but the flatter it

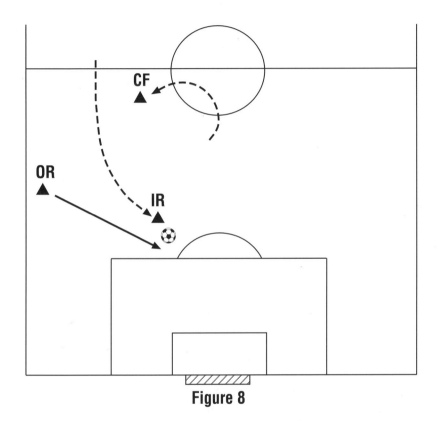

Figure 8

becomes the more the players concerned are taking risks, for the following reasons: (1) they are reducing passing possibilities; and (2) whatever passing possibilities exist in a flat attack, square passing or passing across the field must increase. When square passing increases, the risk of a pass being intercepted increases.

It follows that whatever the number of players involved in attacking play they should pay attention to depth. The resultant formations may resemble squares, diamonds, 'W's or 'M's; this is unimportant. What is important is that the players should understand why depth is necessary.

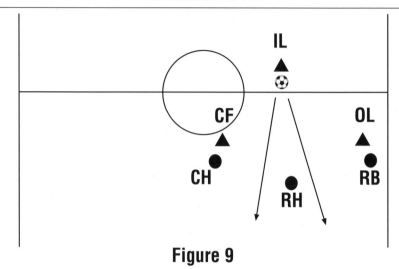

Figure 9

DEPTH IN DEFENSE

Basically the same considerations apply to depth in defense. Here we are involved in restricting space through which and into which attacking players can move with safety. The defense attempts to restrict the gaps through which passes can be made. Players cover not only each other but also the spaces for which the whole defense is responsible.

In *fig.* 9 the three defenders are lying square and thus a pass which beats one of them beats all three. Similarly they are not covering each other and, more important, they are not covering the space into which attacking players wish to move, that is, the space behind them.

In *fig.* 10 the RB and the CH have both moved away from their men in order to give cover against each other and also to threaten the space into which the IL might wish to pass the ball. He can pass to his other forwards but defenders are not beaten by the pass. Defensive structures, therefore, become a series of interlocking triangular formations and the further back they go the tighter they become.

PENETRATION IN ATTACK

The aim of a team which has possession of the ball and is, therefore, in an attacking position is to move the ball as accurately and as quickly as possible into or through the opposing defense. This is assuming that they wish to score since, at times, a team may indulge in interpassing without intending an immediate threat to the opposing goal. Penetrative play can develop in all

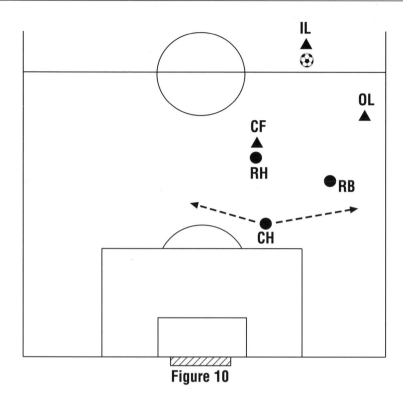

Figure 10

the phases of the game, not only in passes which elude opposing defenders and result in a shot on goal. Indeed, the great teams are able to produce a series of penetrating passes from deep inside their own half, and the more effective their tactics the fewer these passes will be. This is not to say that a team should base its play on long passes into the opposing half of the field; the opposing side would have something to say about this. It should not be overlooked, however, that the more a team plays across the field in its preliminary passing the less effective it will be in penetration.

In *fig.* 11, where an attack has broken down, the goalkeeper has an immediate opportunity to pass the ball to his own OL who has dropped into a deep position. This is a safe pass which rarely achieves anything except ensuring that ball possession is maintained. If the circumstances are right, a pass to the feet of a central attacker (CF or IR) is much more effective. It is made deep into the opposing side and since it is to a central player it may cause a central defender to commit himself to a challenge. The pass to the winger should be the second one for which the goalkeeper looks.

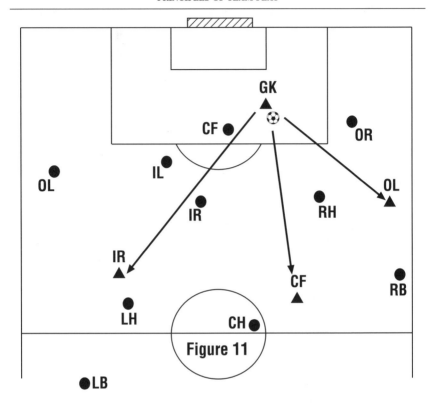

Figure 11

In this situation, it can be right if all members of the side realize and understand the attacking policy. For example, in *fig.* 12, if opposing players are blocking the path for such a pass, the goalkeeper's colleagues must clear the path for him. This particularly applies to players who normally have midfield positions. Two situations are thus created. If opposing players do not move with them the defenders are free to receive a pass. If opposing players do move with them the channel is open for the penetration pass to the advanced forward.

Movements in which players run into positions to decoy players from certain parts of the field in order that more effective passes can be made, are known as 'decoy runs' or 'movements off the ball'. The truly intelligent player is constantly aware of the value of such movements. They are vital if a team is to become an effective attacking unit.

The creation of penetration possibilities becomes more difficult the nearer the attacking side approaches the opponents' goal since the space available for control and the gaps through which passes can be made diminish all the time.

In *fig.* 13 where RH is in possession of the ball, it is obvious that the easy passes to the IL or to the OR achieve very little since the opposing defense is still in a position to watch the ball and attacking players in front of them. In this situation the IL may run on the outside of the opposing RH and away from the center of the field. If his run is well-timed he

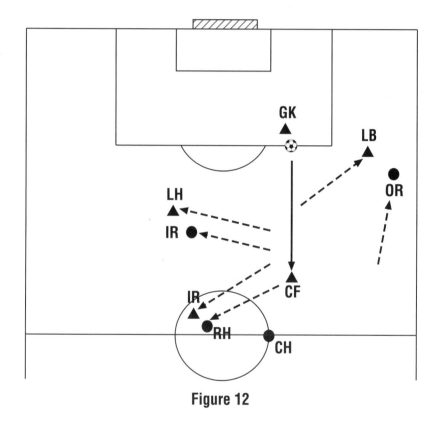

Figure 12

may receive the ball himself, but, more important, he can open up a channel for a pass to the CF. The IR could also assist by drifting out towards the right-wing position thus tempting the LH away from the space in the center of the field. Again he could be considered as a passing possibility but he is helping to clear space for the center-forward which is equally important.

13

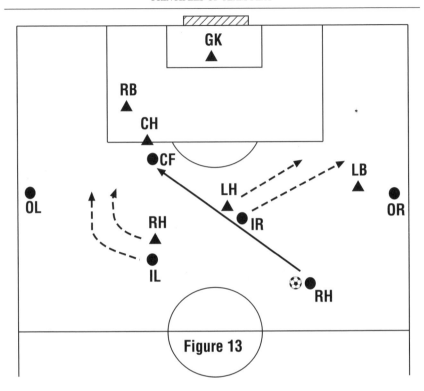

Figure 13

DELAY IN DEFENSE

Where penetration is a major objective in attack, delay must obviously be a principle of defense. This results from a clear understanding of the order of priority for a team which has lost possession of the ball.

The *first* consideration, defensively, is the goal, and this will affect play in every part of the field.

Secondly, having lost the ball, a team must be immediately aware of the space between defending players and, even more important, behind them.

Thirdly, the nearer the attacking side approaches the opposing goal the more closely they must be marked.

It will be easily appreciated from this that time is necessary for the defensive structure to be established. Instead of meeting attacking players, defenders will tend to withdraw to central defensive positions; they will tend to retreat towards their own penalty-area. Advanced players in the team (the forwards mainly) will harass players near to them and will always threaten the line of any pass intended to move the ball towards an advanced and central attacking player on the opposing side. They will try to force the team in possession of the ball to play square or across the field. Mid-field players will tighten up their marking of mid-field attackers while the

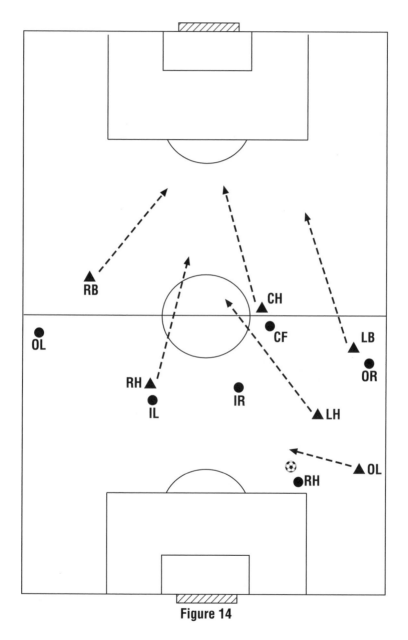

Figure 14

rearmost defenders will adopt covering positions against possible through passes. A team which falls back in front of an opposing side almost inevitably slows it down. In this way the attack is delayed and time for defensive organization is made.

In *fig.* 14 RH has gained possession of the ball. The opposing OL being the nearest player at the time has moved in field to threaten the line of possible passes to attacking forwards. All the rearmost defending players have retreated to central positions. The IR is in a dangerous position hence the need for retreat in order to gain the necessary time for another player to recover. If faced with two players who are free, a defending player, irrespective of his position on the field of play, should always mark or cover the player who is nearer to the goal which is being defended. As far as possible defenders need to see the ball and attackers who are likely to threaten at the same time.

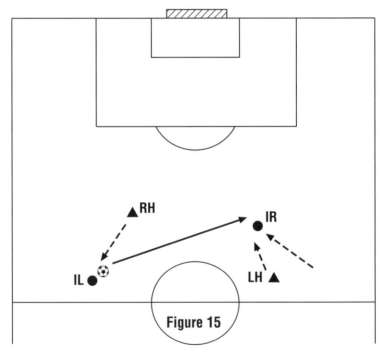

Figure 15

In *fig.* 15 the movement of the RH towards the opposing inside-left, who has the ball, opens the way for a penetration pass from the IL to the IR and the LH has not had time to retreat to a covering position. Here the RH must retreat until he can see both the IL and the IR in front of him. A pass from the IL to the IR, in this situation, does not threaten immediate danger and the LH has time to recover into a position behind the RH (*fig.* 16).

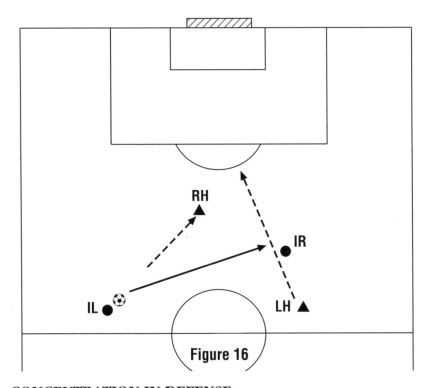

Figure 16

CONCENTRATION IN DEFENSE

From the delaying tactics and the defensive priorities which have been established, it will be obvious that the final stage of defense to be discussed is that within and around the penalty-area. Equally obvious, the area which offers the greatest opportunity for scoring shots is the central part of the penalty-area. Without being too rigid, a reasonable guide to defense can be established as follows. For adult players all shots from 20-25 yards or less present a scoring threat to the defending side. It may also be said that the finer the angle of the shot, the less likely it is to score.

Two imaginary lines projecting outwards, one from each goal post, at an angle of 45° to the goal-line, and approximately 30-35 yards in length (*fig.* 17), enclose the central zone of defense. If the foremost defenders are on the outer edge of this zone, the possibility of shots being taken from less than 30-35 yards is reduced; and if defenders are concentrated within this arc we

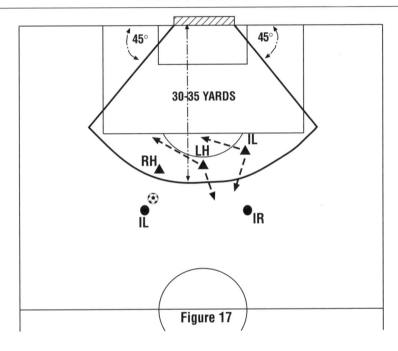

Figure 17

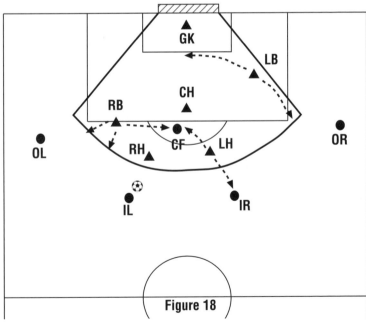

Figure 18

can expect few angled shots to score since we have narrowed the angle. This is, perhaps, an over-simplification, but it will serve as a rough guide.

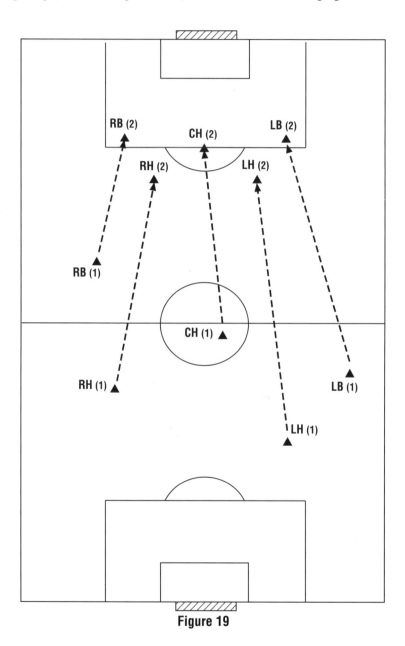

Figure 19

Just as a goalkeeper's job is governed by angles, so all defenders must take into account the angle of attack.

In *fig.* 18 the 3-2 zone defense is designed to produce maximum coverage against scoring opportunities in the most dangerous part of the field. We have already seen how necessary delay is in defensive organization and how defenders, when they are in doubt, retreat centrally and, as a result, concentrate centrally in front of goal. This retreat or withdrawal from wide positions to concentrated central defensive positions is known as 'funnelling in defense'.

In *fig.* 19 from wide positions in mid-field defenders converge into concentrated central positions in and outside the penalty-area. This concentration of players not only keeps shooting opportunities at a reasonably ineffective range but also reduces the space between defending players. This makes the exploitation of a through-pass very difficult and also allows attacking players very little time in which to control and manoeuvre the ball should such a pass reach them.

WIDTH IN ATTACK

If on the one hand defenders retreat and concentrate effectively, every attempt must be made in the attacking half of the field to tempt the

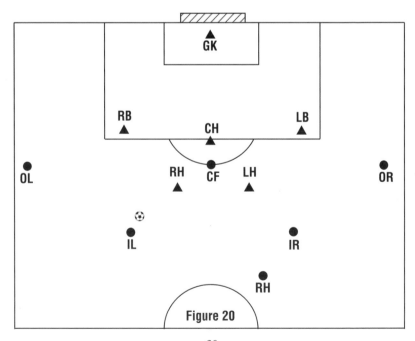

Figure 20

20

defenders away from concentrated defensive positions. This can only be achieved if the attacking side has passing opportunities over the whole width of the field.

In *fig.* 20 the defending side is retreating and concentrating. If the attacking players, particularly on the wings, follow them into the space outside the penalty-area, they will make this space even more restricted than it is. By having players in wide positions the attack may tempt defending players away from central positions. This particularly applies where one or more defenders have a liking for the physical challenge. Players of this type take risks in order to be in a position to tackle for the ball: they therefore take up positions slightly nearer to whichever of the attacking players are in their particular sector of the defense.

It is an inescapable fact that however well-organized a defense may be, and however restrained the individual players within it, human nature still plays its part. Any group of players who are subjected to the physical and psychological pressure of attack for long periods will tend to become anxious. A defending side is only relaxed if it succeeds in regaining possession of the ball within a reasonable space of time, and the longer this time lasts

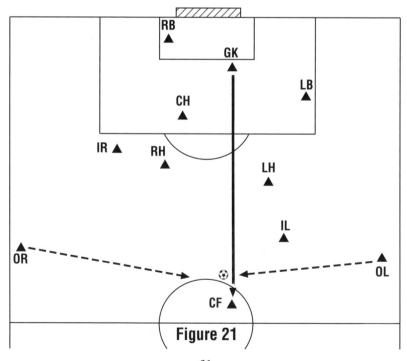

Figure 21

the less relaxed and confident they become. The less confident they become the greater the risks which they may be tempted to take. Psychological pressure is thus a factor which must be allowed for in all tactical considerations.

In a system of play which may be heavily defensive, width in attack may seem to be not so necessary. There is little point in having two players wide on the touch lines when a team plays with three forwards for the greater part of the game. When the ball is released from defense it is, initially, far more important that the receiving player shall obtain immediate support. In this situation both wingers may move quickly to support the center-forward, or one winger and the center-forward may move across field to support the second winger as in *fig*. 21 and 22. Here the immediate concern is to

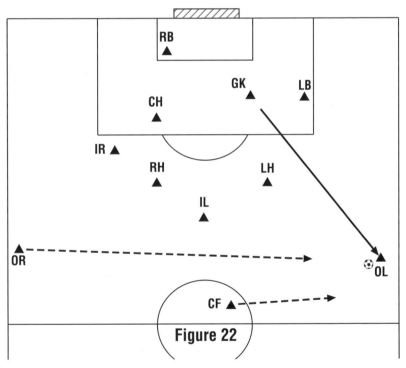

Figure 22

provide whatever support in depth is possible for the benefit of the player receiving the ball. Since a three-man attack is at a heavy numerical disadvantage they will try to minimize the disadvantage by all moving to a more restricted part of the field. By doing this they may also cause the opposing defense to move over thus creating an opportunity for width to be re-established by players who break out from defense quickly on the flanks, (*fig.* 23). In other words by loading their attack on one side of the field they create the possibility of a break-through on that side, but they also create a

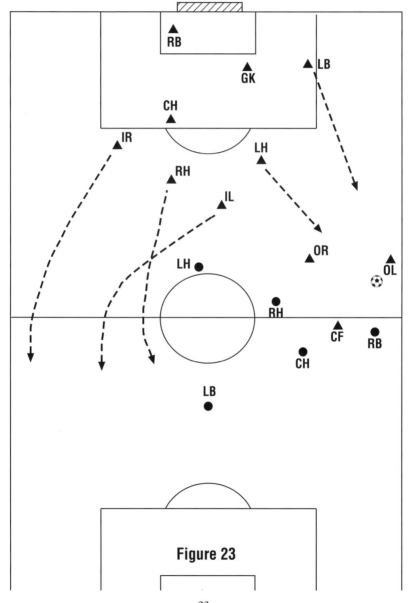

Figure 23

chance for players to adopt effective wide positions on the far side of the field.

This generalization on width in attack is much more applicable to the preparation or building-up phase of attacking play. When a team is attempting to strike at goal, chances have to be taken and decisions made quickly. In this phase of the game however, width should be maintained and, if lost, re-established as quickly as possible.

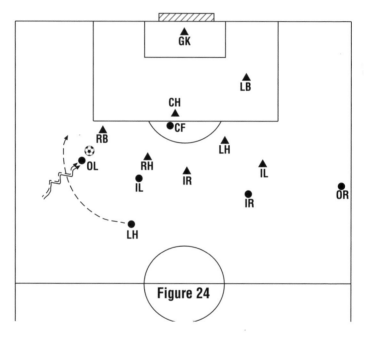

Figure 24

In *fig.* 24 the attacking side is faced with a concentrated and balanced defense. The OL has moved in-field to attack the right flank of the defense and he has thus narrowed the attacking front. The attack is well supported and the LH has run outside his own OL. He has thus created an overlap and threatens to turn the flank of the defense. At this stage the OL can continue to attack along his original line but the defense and particularly covering defenders must be aware of the threat which is created by the LH's wide run.

MOBILITY IN ATTACK

From the examples used to illustrate the necessity for delay and concentration in defense, it is apparent that defensive play lends itself to easy organization. A defending team is waiting for mistakes; it may, at the same time, actively encourage the opposing side to make them. Provided that there is a clear understanding of priorities, the defensive organization of a team can be simple and yet extremely effective in its simplicity. This can be easily proved by allowing eight or nine players to attack a goal which is defended by four or five players. The number of scoring shots will be very few, indeed the number of shooting attempts may even be low. This is because the attack is within reach of goal which demands precision and care. The defense is concerned with merely stopping the attack and, therefore, their work demands less accuracy; they can merely kick the ball out of play, a tactic crude but remarkably effective.

In attacking play, too much organization can be restrictive. As players are faced with the problems created by a defense, they must be allowed to experiment with solutions. They will have a basic attacking plan and they may well have 'set' or rehearsed plays, but they must be encouraged to react naturally and intelligently to new problems.

One of the means employed to disturb a defense is to continually change the positions of the attacking players. A defender who is dealing with the

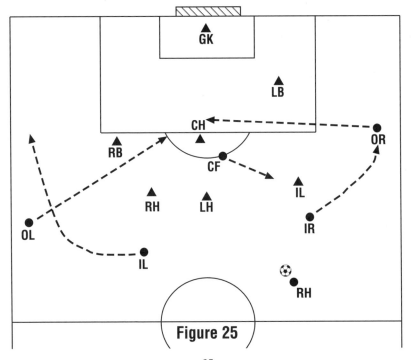

Figure 25

25

same opponent in the same part of the field for the whole game has a relatively easy task, and he learns far more about the attacker's play than the attacker learns about his. This is a natural consequence of the negative side of defensive play. Defenders faced with different opponents interchanging their positions intelligently are often puzzled.

This is best illustrated by the use of diagonal running and overlap running by an attacking side which is trying to deal with a well organized and concentrated defense on the edge of that defenses penalty-area. Here are some of the interchanges which might be effective in *fig.* 25 where the RH has the ball: the OR moves across field to the CF position, the CF has moved towards the IR position to offer himself as a target for RH's pass; it is likely that the CH will have followed him and thus the interchange between himself and the OR could leave the OR as the new center-forward and relatively free from a defender. Similarly, the IR could assist by running outside the OR; he has then cleared space for the center-forward should the RH wish to pass to him. The OL may have decided to try a diagonal run behind the CH either for a pass or to create a diversion by drawing attention to himself. The IL could then run outside the full-back perhaps taking an opposing central

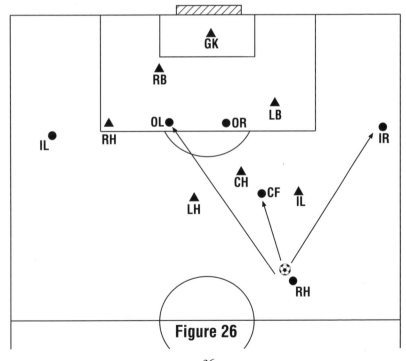

Figure 26

26

defender with him and also re-establishing wide passing possibilities in attack. We now have an attack with players in the positions shown in *fig.* 26. The employment of diagonal movements achieves two purposes. The *first*, as we have seen, is to shake the confidence of defenders by surprising them. The *second* is concerned with space; all the movements of attacking players near the penalty-area have to be watched closely and judged quickly by defenders. They are never quite certain whether a player is moving to receive a pass or to tempt a defender away from a position in which some other attacker may receive it.

The most refined use of the skill of diagonal running occurs when the player can run into positions in which he is an immediate danger himself; should he receive the ball, and in which, at the same time, he has opened up the possibility of a pass to someone who is just as dangerously placed. A further generalization on diagonal running is that the nearer the attack comes to its opponents' final defensive positions, the flatter the angle of the run must be.

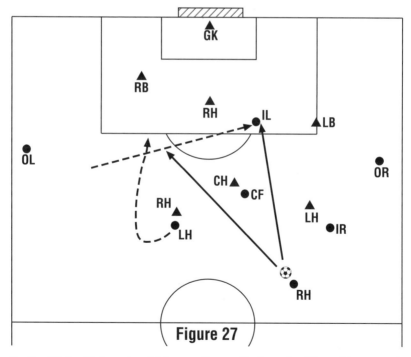

Figure 27

In *fig.* 27 the IL has timed his run diagonally into the IR position to coincide with the turn and run of the LH. For the opposing RH, choice of action is difficult. Should he follow the IL and block the threat to the goal or should he cover the threat which is posed by the run of the LH.

It will also be seen that the more direct is the run towards goal the more positive must be the reaction of a defender. A straight run towards goal by an attacker must be covered. In other words, the problem of a choice of action is solved for the defender. Naturally, such a run, if it is successful, usually results in a goal scoring chance. The conclusion to be drawn is that the more all the forwards adopt this kind of attacking run, the more easily the attack will be stopped.

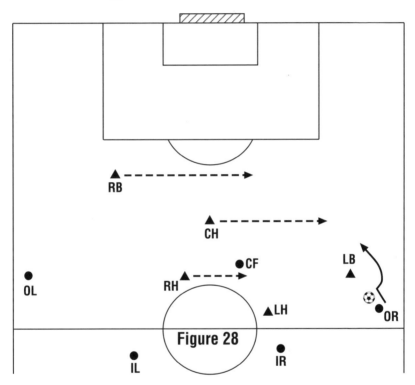

Figure 28

BALANCE IN DEFENSE

From the analysis of the need for mobility in attack it is apparent that defensive play is concerned with the maintenance of cover at all times. If the movement of attacking players is calculated to draw defenders out of position in order to free other attackers, and also to create attacking space, then the defense must be balanced against these threats. Attacking play aims at getting through, around, or over defensive players and thus any lack of balance in defensive organization will allow these aims to be achieved.

Let us take the diagonal system of covering which used the two full-backs and the center-half as its key units.

In *fig.* 28 where play is developing on the LB's side of the field, cover can be afforded by both CH and RB if the LB is beaten. If the CF moves out to the wing behind the LB he is threatening to unbalance the defense. If the defensive organization is good then the LB may leave his opposing winger and mark the player who has taken up the new wing position (the CF) in *fig.* 29.

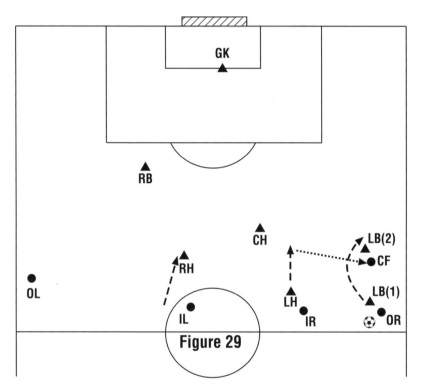

Figure 29

This means that the cover is still intact and the defense is still balanced against a breakthrough on the left side of the field. If the CH follows the CF out to the wing, however, cover remains but balance is destroyed immediately (*fig.* 30).

A large space has been created in mid-field which can become an immediate passage to goal. The RB can move across to check this threat but now the same amount of space has been left on his defensive flank. We can also see how the same situation may affect the positions of the wing-half in this defensive structure.

In *fig.* 31 the RH has dropped back to fill the gap left by the CH and has

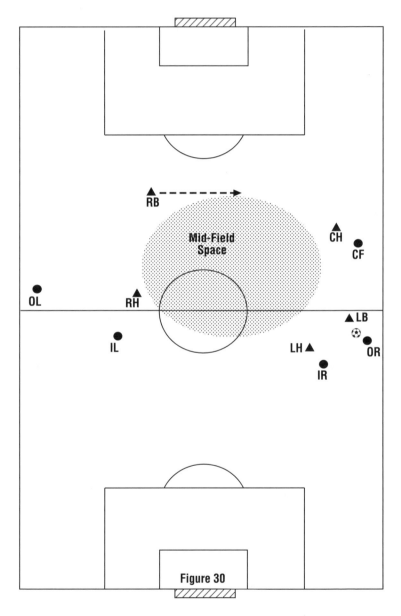

Figure 30

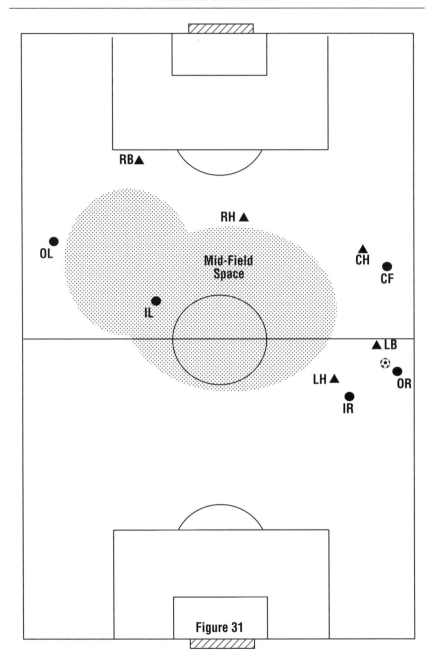

Figure 31

thus re-established balance at the rear of the defense At the same time, however, his new role has left a large space in the inside-left position which may be exploited if play can be switched from right to left quickly enough. If this exploitation is quick and accurate, it will cause one or the other of the defenders on that side of the field to be drawn out of position. It is now obvious how delay will be necessary in order that balance can be re-established.

It is not uncommon for attackers to be tightly marked by defenders, particularly when a sides tactical plan is based upon stopping one outstanding attacking player. Where such a player finds himself subjected to tight marking throughout the game he knows that his access to the ball will be severely limited. Thus, he will try to take the opposing defender into positions where his absence from the final defensive positions may cause the maximum

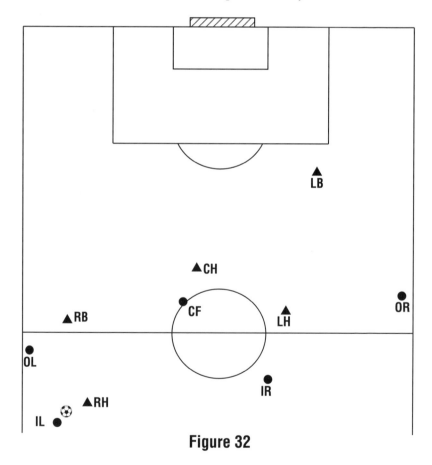

Figure 32

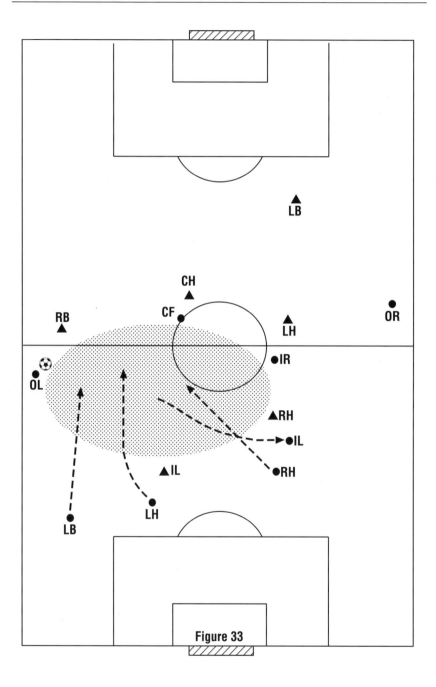

Figure 33

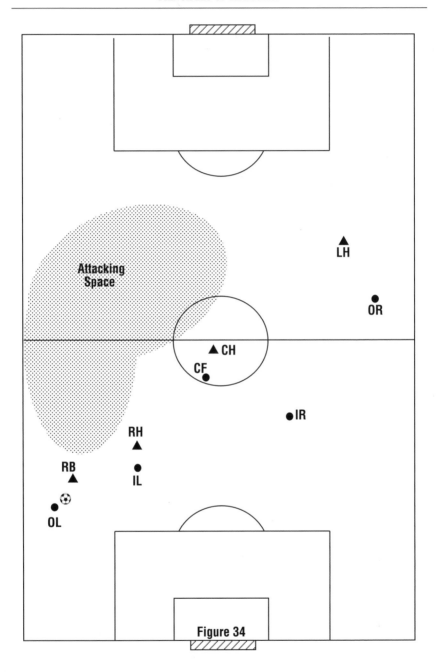

Figure 34

amount of trouble. Let us imagine an inside-forward who is receiving close attention from an opposing wing-half. If he merely moves into other forward positions he will be followed by the wing-half and the rest of the defenders will cover accordingly.

In *fig.* 32 the IL has moved into a wing position and the defensive balance remains intact.

In *fig.* 33 the IL has moved wide and deep into his own half and virtually joined his own right-half. If the space thus created between the opposing RH and the other defenders can be exploited these defenders can be drawn. This may be achieved by a temporary change of positions whereby the IL now becomes the right-half and the right-half moves into an attacking role. The use of a deep lying center-forward in setting problems for the rigid stopper center-half achieved the same effect. These problems will always be created for defenders who are used in tight, man-for-man marking duties. In the same way the use of one wing-man as the principle link player between attack and defense is aimed at destroying the balance of a defense.

In *fig.* 34 if the RB moves to mark the OL he leaves a great deal of space unguarded behind him. If the right-half is detailed to mark the OL, space is again left within the defensive structure. One method used to counter the use of a deep lying wing-man involves a return to the system of play which was widespread before the introduction of the present offside-law. Wing-halves marked wingers and full-backs marked inside forwards.

In conclusion, therefore, we may say that the more rigid the man-for-man marking duties of defenders become, the more likely it is that the defense will become unbalanced. Marking space is much more important than marking players. The nearer one moves towards one's own goal the more the two objectives become the same thing. In and outside its own penalty-area a team aims at restricting space and also the free movement of attackers. It is still true, however, that even in this situation space can provide a bigger problem than attackers.

CONTROL AND RESTRAINT IN DEFENSE

Consideration of depth, delay, and balance in defense means an emphasis on restraint in this aspect of the game. Defensive play necessitates a high awareness of risk and the priorities which must be recognized when the opposing side has possession of the ball. Players who are defensively employed, and this means the whole of a team when possession has been lost, must pay close attention to their function relative to all the other players in the team. For example, if a winger loses possession of the ball to an

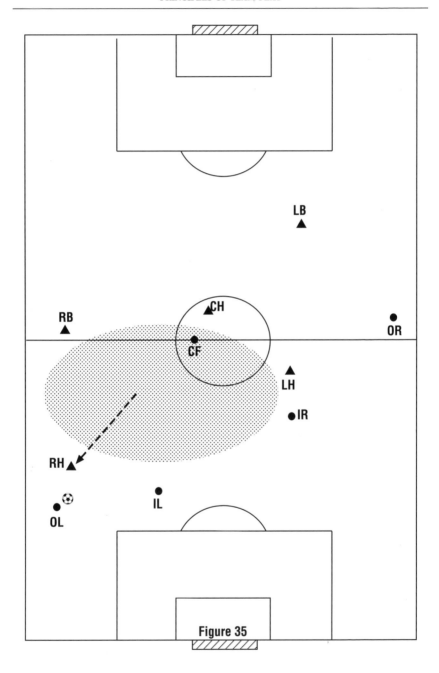

Figure 35

36

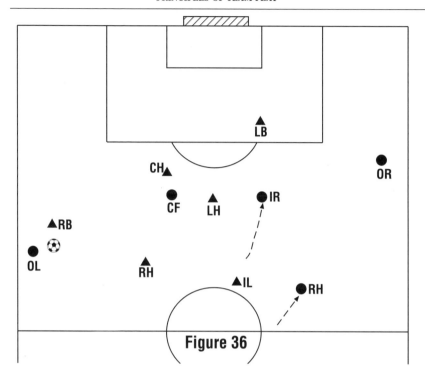

Figure 36

opposing full-back, perhaps in a position close to the full-back's own goal line, a wild challenge which enables the full-back to beat him is bad defensive play on the winger's part. The challenge may have been spectacular but the mere fact that the full-back beats the winger is enough to expose other members of the defending side.

The higher the level of soccer the more likely it is that the side with the ball will be able to take advantage of such weaknesses. There are certain examples of lack of restraint in defensive play which typify the problems involved. The first is the player who is always drawn towards the ball. This might be the RH in *fig.* 35 who, finding himself nearer to the OL than his own RB, is drawn out to make a challenge. In being drawn he exposes a gap between himself, the CH and the LH. The RB dare not move forward to fill the space since by doing so he will leave space behind both himself and the RH. If he moves forward he and the right-half will be square for a short time and therefore open to penetration. Control is shown by the RH when he falls back into a normal defensive position where he can watch developments as they occur, in front of him. The winger with the ball is not an immediate threat since all defensive players are balanced in covering roles. In exactly the same way the center-forward who rushes towards the goalkeeper, chasing a through pass which he has no hope of catching, shows no restraint. Having drawn the CF, the goalkeeper can immediately set up play to one of his defenders who will in turn cause another opposing player to be drawn.

A second factor influencing the stability of a defense is the extent to which players watch the ball. In defense the restriction of space is of major importance and particularly, as we have seen, space between and behind defensive players. The danger in watching the ball, especially when it is not within playing range, is that attackers can move onto the 'blindside' of defenders and into spaces behind them. A natural consequence of ball watching is that the player forgets his defensive responsibilities and tends to react to the movement of the ball.

In *fig.* 36, where the ball is held by the OL, the IR has moved onto the blind side of the defending LH. This is the side of the player furthest away from the ball. In the event of play being switched by a cross-field pass. the defending LB is caught between two players. In the same way the attacking RH is threatening to move onto the blind side of the defending IL. Attackers can only achieve this when the defenders' attention is drawn towards the ball. It follows that defenders should always be aware of those attackers who are trying to move behind them.

Football is, in many respects, a test of patience. Defenders restrain themselves in order that when they challenge, they either stand a very good chance of getting the ball themselves or other defenders stand a good chance of getting it. In attack, a team tests the patience of the defending side by tempting defenders to make a badly calculated challenge. It is fairly true to say that the nearer play moves towards the penalty-area the greater the degree of control and restraint which must be exercised by defending players.

IMPROVISATION IN ATTACK

Since modern defensive play is highly organized, methods of attack must be unlimited. The tactical use of a team's strengths in attack is, of course, important but their rigid application is erroneous. When an attacking player with the ball is faced by an opponent, the decision as to how to beat him is entirely with the attacker. He will have tried to assess the various strengths and weaknesses of the opposing defenders, and although a great deal of information may be available about individual opposing players before a match commences, it will be only a fragment of the knowledge required to ensure that they are beaten regularly. If it were possible to acquire fullest knowledge of players in the opposing team, the problem of coaching a team to combine effectively against them would be greatly simplified.

For example, a team may have decided that its attacking strength is in the ability of its wingers to beat opposing full-backs on the outside. The basic attacking plan might be to isolate opposing full-backs, leaving the winger to attack the full-back alone. Crossfield passes might also be used from the inside-forward and the wing-halves to try to use the winger's speed. This is fine, as an attacking formation, but in a game one of the wingers may find that he is more easily able to beat the full-back on the inside. If this is so the attack must be adaptable enough to exploit this alternative .

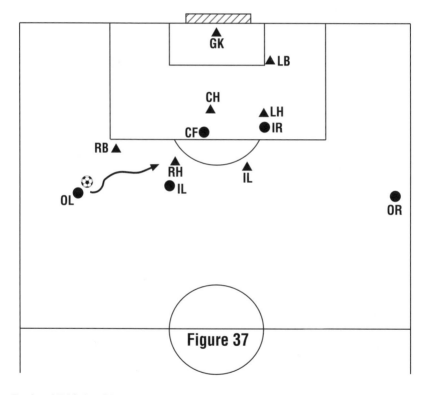

Figure 37

In *fig.* 37 if the OL moves inside his full-back he will merely move into an area already congested by players. The aim of his other forwards will be to clear the area for him and create better opportunities to exploit the full-back's weakness.

In *fig.* 38 the attacking IL has run diagonally across the RB thus attempting to draw the RH into a covering position behind the RB. Both the attacking CF and his IR have attempted to move behind their opponents thus trying to draw them away from the center of the field. The OR has moved away from the opposing LB in order to retain depth. This full-back is now concerned with his covering responsibilities towards the center of the field and he also has to be aware of the possibility of the ball being played to the OR.

To overcome organized defensive play, a great deal of movement is required from opposing attackers to commit the defenders to false positions. Some of the movement will be to receive passes but a great deal of it will be aimed at creating opportunities for other attackers.

One of the most important skills which any player can possess is the ability to take on and beat an opponent with the ball. This skill is just as important to a full-back as it is to a winger, yet it is far too often ignored in the coaching of players at all levels. Whenever and wherever an opponent is beaten the player who has been successful has created difficulties for the opposing defense. He has established a position where the attacking side has

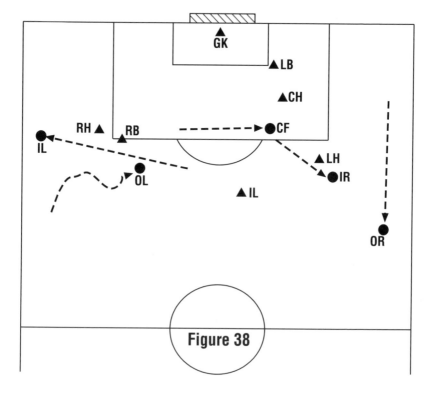

Figure 38

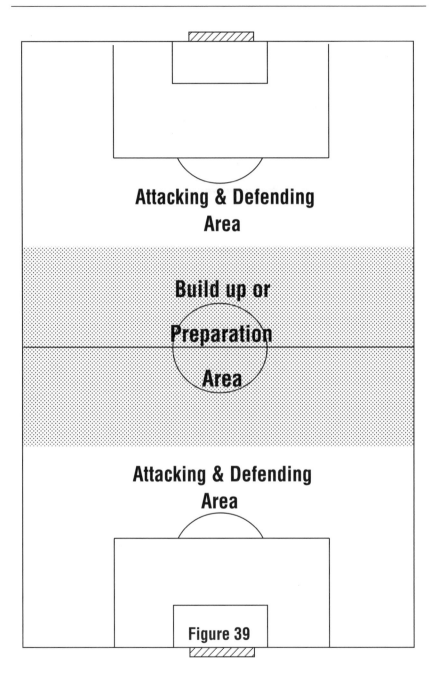

Attacking & Defending Area

Build up or Preparation Area

Attacking & Defending Area

Figure 39

a spare man! The use of situations in the game where an attacking side has one or more players spare is a most important aspect of attacking soccer and one to which a great deal of attention must be given in coaching and training. In the final attacking phase of the game, that is to say just outside and inside the opponents' penalty area, the ability of an attacker to dribble and beat an opposing defender is of great value. This is a part of the field where defenders must tackle with care since a careless tackle can result in the award of a penalty-kick. It follows, therefore, that players who are gifted in their ability to dribble around an opponent should reserve this ability for that part of the field where it is likely to be most effective. To show all one's tricks in mid-field is to give opposing players too much information and in this less dangerous area the defenders will learn far more than the attackers.

Generally speaking, the field can be divided into three areas (*fig.* 39). The attacking area is the one in which, for example, wingers capable of taking on a full-back will be most effective. It is occasionally true that quick, attacking breaks from deep defensive positions are successful. This particularly applies where a team supports its attack heavily and where its defenders are drawn into square positions. Here they leave the maximum amount of space behind them into which the ball can be played and into which opposing forwards can move. Today, however, when teams are much more aware of space and tend to restrict it very quickly when opponents have the ball, this attacking move has to be used sparingly. This assumes, of course, that the so-called long-passing game or the short-passing game represent two extremes. A good team will use both according to the play of their opponents. To use a succession of short passes emphasizes accuracy but lacks speed. Where there is the possibility for a long, accurate pass in achieving penetration this should be used. Obviously, to build the whole of an attacking system upon the long pass is emphasizing speed and directness at the expense of control and accuracy. There can be no simple solution to attacking problems, but players must be encouraged to consider the variety of ways by which a defense or a defender may be exposed.

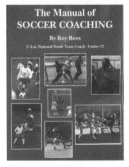